Original title:
Alchemy of Leaves

Copyright © 2025 Creative Arts Management OÜ
All rights reserved.

Author: Micah Sterling
ISBN HARDBACK: 978-1-80566-668-4
ISBN PAPERBACK: 978-1-80566-953-1

Secrets Buried in Autumn's Embrace

In piles of crackling gold they lay,
Squirrels plotting their winter buffet.
Leaves whisper secrets, oh, such glee,
As they dance in circles, wild and free.

Acorns giggle, their hats all askew,
A nutty ballet, what more can they do?
While trees shake off their leafy attire,
Mother Nature's joke, a comedic choir.

Enchantment of the Withering Woods

Dancing twigs and pirouetting roots,
Flipping through shadows like clumsy brutes.
Mushrooms chuckle in their earthy crowns,
As branches sweep low, wearing leafy frowns.

The woods tease us with their moaning sighs,
As leaves discuss juicy autumnal pies.
A fox does a jig, then smirks with delight,
In this comedy play, oh what a sight!

Paintbrushes of Wind and Water

The paintbrushes swirl in the brisk cool air,
Each gust of wind brings a mischievous flair.
Raindrops giggle, sneaking past the trees,
Tickling the bark with a cheeky breeze.

Rippling puddles reflect silly hats,
And all the critters share chitchat with rats.
Colors of fall splash with a giggly cheer,
Nature's own canvas, oh so sincere!

Fall's Final Flourish

One last show, the leaves start their fall,
Spinning and twirling, like a carnival ball.
They crack jokes as they drop with a thud,
Creating a carpet, now splashed with good mud.

The wind plays a tune, a flirty refrain,
While pumpkins roll by, quite proud of their gain.
With laughter and mischief, the season takes flight,
As autumn waves goodbye, what a hilarious sight!

Harmonies of the Harvest

In the fields where veggies giggle,
Potatoes dance, while greens do wiggle.
Corn sings a tune of sunny delight,
Radishes jive with all their might.

Tomatoes try to steal the show,
While squash does nothing, just lays low.
Carrots rhyme with their leafy flair,
As pumpkins pull off jumpy air.

Melodies in the Maple

When leaves turn gold, it's quite the scene,
Squirrels grooving, a fluffy routine.
Maple syrup flows with a sweet, sweet beat,
While birds drop notes from their leafy seat.

The wind joins in, a playful breeze,
Tickling trees like they're on a tease.
Chirping crickets add their sound,
Making nature's band quite profound.

Rituals of the Earth

In the garden, gnomes spin around,
Digging treasures from underground.
Worms wiggle, while seeds take a leap,
Making promises they'll keep.

The sun winks down with a golden grin,
As daisies hold hands, a floral spin.
Earthworms whisper secrets shared,
While daisies don't mind being ensnared.

Foliage and the Flicker

Leaves flicker like they've lost their mind,
Playing hide and seek with the wind so blind.
A rustle here, a twirl over there,
They break into giggles without a care.

Breezes tease with a gentle push,
Trees sway back with a playful hush.
Foliage fans, an audience cheering,
As nature's jokes leave us all leering.

Symphony of the Decay

In the garden where laughter grows,
Leaves like dancers strike silly poses.
A rustle, a tumble, they prance away,
Nature's own version of a cabaret.

Crinkly edges, like old folks' tales,
Whispering secrets, where humor prevails.
Golden hues wearing their best attire,
While worms in tuxedos dream of the choir.

Shades of Renewal

Faded browns with a splash of green,
Leaves gossip about what they've seen.
A curious breeze with a wink and a tease,
Turns giggles from trees into hearty wheezes.

Saplings poke fun at their older kin,
With youthful banter, they spin and grin.
Each drop of rain a joke from the sky,
As puns sprout and tumble, oh my, oh my!

The Heartbeat of Rustling Leaves

Leaves chatter in twilight, a flirt and a tease,
Tickling the branches with giggles in the breeze.
Swaying together in a playful ballet,
They bump and they jive, come join in the fray.

Each crunch underfoot a laugh in disguise,
A cacophony of chuckles beneath autumn skies.
As squirrels pretend to be masters of flight,
The leaves just roll over, they find it a delight.

Enchanted Boughs

Branches stretch out, with a wink and a nudge,
Inviting the sun, saying, "Come be our judge!"
Foliage whispering jokes to the air,
While shadows play tag with a flair so rare.

The acorns, they giggle, as they drop on the ground,
Making a symphony of the softest sound.
Each leaf, a comedian in colorful coats,
Telling tales where laughter and nature promotes.

Echoes of Decaying Splendor

Once golden crowns now tattered rags,
Whispers of laughter in rustling hags.
Squirrels giggle, planning their heist,
To snag the last acorn, they're not being nice.

Leaves tumble down like jokes on the floor,
Each one a punchline, but we want more.
Gathering chuckles in piles so bright,
Mischief in shadows, delight in spite.

Transmutation Underneath the Bark

A tree has secrets, it's quite the tease,
Barking out laughter as I scratch with ease.
Under the surface, it's quite the show,
Splitting wide open to let humor flow.

Worms are the jesters, wriggling with glee,
Turning our scraps into a grand spree.
Mushrooms pop up like surprise guests at night,
In their fungal costumes, they dance with delight.

Shadows of the Shifting Seasons

Summer slides out with a sunburnt grin,
While autumn slips in, wearing a spin.
Pumpkins chuckle, spilling their seeds,
Tickling the ground as nature proceeds.

Snowflakes fumble, they trip and they fall,
Winter's cold breath makes everyone stall.
Yet spring springs forth with a wobbly leap,
Proclaiming the blossoms, now you've had sleep!

Fragments of Time in Every Leaf

In little green notes, time pens its play,
Crinkled and toasted in a curious way.
They flutter and twist like hands on a clock,
Tickling the air as they dance on the block.

Each leaf has a tale, a quirk or a twist,
To read them aloud would certainly assist.
With shades of laughter in every hue,
Nature's confetti, a comedic view.

Remnants of the Emerald

In the garden, a leaf danced,
Hoping for a chance to prance.
A snail said, 'Not so fast, my friend!'
You're not winning any race to the end.

Beneath a branch, a squirrel stashed,
A treasure trove of nuts he'd crashed.
But wait! What's that? A leaf fell down,
His prize turned into leafy crown!

The wind came by, and with a laugh,
Swirled leaves like a silly gaffe.
The acorns giggled, took a spin,
In this leafy jest, how can we win?

So let us toast to green abound,
With funny tales in leaves we've found.
For every fall and twist we see,
Is just the nature's humor spree!

Tinctures of Time and Nature

Once a leaf, so bold and bright,
Decided to start a funny fight.
With autumn's flair, it called the wind,
'You pick the side, it's not a sin!'

Old bark chuckled, full of rings,
'Time's a jester, oh how it sings!'
A bee buzzed by, with gossip keen,
'Leafy drama, a joke unseen?'

The sun peeked through, a cheeky grin,
'Leave your worries, let joy begin!'
As shadows fluttered, the jokes grew loud,
In nature's theater, oh how we bowed!

With every hue, the truth would flash,
Leaves in laughter, in a fiery clash.
Each day a potion, brewed with delight,
In the garden's embrace, all is bright!

Sculpted by the Seasons

Springtime giggled with sprightly greens,
While winter teased with icy sheens.
Autumn chuckled, a burst of fire,
As summer danced, a leaf's desire.

While branches sway and roots entwine,
Each season tells a joke divine.
Under the sun, they spin and weave,
In a caper where no one believes!

Leaves, like jesters, bring the cheer,
Shuffling colors, loud and clear.
A maple shouted, 'Catch my hue!'
As others followed in silly rue.

In nature's play, the jokes collide,
With little critters giggling wide.
For every twist the seasons bring,
Is a comedic leaf-laden fling!

A Tonic of Transition

The leaves whispered secrets in the breeze,
With every rustle, they aimed to tease.
'This summer tan won't last for long,'
Said a leaf that thought it sang a song.

Golds and reds lined up in a row,
'Last leaf standing will steal the show!'
Said one with pride, but the wind just swirled,\nAnd
tossed it high, much to its chagrin, it twirled.

Branches held meetings, plotting schemes,
Of who would land in fall's rich dreams.
Each flake of color, a comedy fare,
As nature painted jokes everywhere.

So raise a glass to leaves on the move,
With every chuckle, they groove and prove.
In this whimsical tunic of hues,
Transition cheers, with every leaf that snooze!

Whispers of the Autumn Breeze

The winds come laughing through the trees,
They play with branches, tease the bees.
Squirrels in chase, they leap and bound,
As leaves swirl near, a crisp delight found.

A fox in a jacket, stylish and sleek,
Winks at the leaves, so bright and unique.
"Catch me if you can!" he sprightly calls,
As acorns join in, doing their falls.

Caterpillars don hats, quite dapper and neat,
While crickets play tunes with a rhythm so sweet.
The world's a stage, every creature a star,
In this merry show, we all raise the bar.

So let's join the fun, in this leafy charade,
With giggles and spins, as autumn parade.
For the breeze is a jester, the trees take a bow,
In nature's own circus, let's join in now!

Secrets in the Maple's Veins

Maples whisper secrets, oh what a thrill,
In their leafy hearts, stories to spill.
They chuckle at changes, hues of delight,
Painting the world, from morning to night.

Birch trees gossip with a rustling sound,
While pine needles giggle, falling all around.
"What's your color today? Let's see who's grand!"
Said the reds to the yellows, both lively and bland.

The sap runs sticky, like a candy-coated stream,
As squirrels debate which nut is supreme.
"Maple syrup for brunch!" a young bird proclaims,
"But you better not spill it! Or we'll all rue the names!"

So gather your friends for this colorful joke,
With leaves as our laughter, the woods will revive.
In the branches above, stories twist and weave,
As secrets unfold in the breaths of the leaves.

The Dance of Gold and Crimson

A dancer in crimson twirls on the breeze,
With a laugh so hearty, she's sure to please.
Gold leaves join in, with a shimmy and shake,
Their party of colors, the ground they awake.

In this playful ballet, the branches all cheer,
"Let's leap and spin! Autumn's finally here!"
The grass rolls away, trying not to laugh,
As each leaf takes flight, on their whimsical path.

A troupe of bright acorns prepares for their show,
While a walnut attempts an elegant throw.
"Look at me! I'm fabulous!" one pebble claims proud,
But trip on a leaf? Oh no, that's not allowed!

As day turns to dusk, in a glimmering waltz,
Nature's own dancers take spins and somersaults.
With laughter unending and joy to behold,
The dance floors of autumn are vibrant and bold.

Transformation at Dusk

At dusk, the leaves gather for a grand chat,
With rumors of change, they drop their old hat.
"I'll be bright orange!" one leaf starts to boast,
While another declares, "I'll be the most!"

The moon peeks in, with a mischievous grin,
"What's cooking, leaves? Let the fun begin!"
A walnut grins wide, casting dreams all around,
"Let's transform this twilight into laughter unbound!"

Ghostly swirls come, turning the trees thin,
With shadows prancing, let the games begin.
Each leaf blinks twice, with a giggle, they toss,
Falling like feathers; who knows who's the boss?

So take off your coats, new colors await,
Sprouted in laughter, they dance out of fate.
As dusk whispers softly, a new tale will bloom,
In the land of the leaves, there's always more room!

Nature's Gold in Autumn

Crisp air whispers softly, trees start to crack,
Leaves drop like coins, nature's little snack.
Squirrels hoard treasure, they plot and they scheme,
Jumping through branches, it's all in their dream.

Pumpkins are grinning, faces carved with glee,
Scarecrows are laughing, a rowdy spree.
Wind makes a mockery, rustles the scene,
Nature's a prankster, oh what a routine!

Golden hues dance in the twilight's embrace,
Even the crows join the seasonal race.
Nature's confetti falls, a whimsical surprise,
Foliage frolics, under cloud-baked skies.

So here's to the laughter, the colors we cheer,
Autumn's a jester, spreading good cheer.
Gather 'round folks, for a seasonal toast,
To funny old nature, we love the most!

Secrets of the Forest Floor

Under the leaves where the mushrooms reside,
Creatures make mischief, they've got nowhere to hide.
Twirling in shadows, a parade unseen,
In hush-hush whisperings, they gather keen.

Worms wear their suits, made of dirt and delight,
While rabbits play poker deep into the night.
Tiny ants hitch a ride on a wandering snail,
This underground circus never goes pale.

Pinecone acorns plotting their grand escape,
Trees gossip softly, weaving a cape.
The forest floor chuckles, a hidden delight,
It revels in secrets, a merry old sight.

So dance with the critters, nature's delight,
Join in the laughter that echoes through night.
Artistry hidden, like jewels in a chest,
In the depths of the woodlands, we find laughter's rest!

The Dance of Dying Foliage

Leaves take a bow, they're ready to go,
Twirling and swirling, a colorful show.
Dancing in circles, they let out a cheer,
In a final performance, they vanish from here.

Oh, those flamboyant hues—red, gold, and brown,
As the trees don their coats, they'll never frown.
With a rustle of laughter, they tip and they sway,
Each leaf a performer, joining the fray.

They slip on the pavement, all smooth and so sly,
A comic ballet beneath the blue sky.
Neighbors all chuckle, as they sweep and they rake,
Who knew those leaves could be such a flake?

So here's to the foliage, with humor galore,
Let's celebrate fall, as they dance and explore.
In the crisp autumn air, we laugh and we sing,
For the grand finale that nature will bring!

Magician of the Seasons

A hat full of colors and tricks up his sleeve,
The seasons are sprightly, you'd better believe.
With a flick of his wrist, winter's chill's in place,
Then spring steals the show, brings a fresh, lively grace.

Summer's a hotshot, with a sunbeam or two,
As wildflowers bloom, in a brilliant debut.
Then autumn with laughter, in gold might appear,
With playful leaves tossing without any fear.

He conjures up storms, makes the wind do a jig,
While rainbows play tag, oh it's really quite big!
A potion of sunshine, a sprinkle of gloom,
With nature's sly magic, we find ourselves home.

So watch this magician, with awe and with glee,
He turns up the seasons like clever esprit.
In the great show of life, he's the jester supreme,
The seasons are funny, fulfilling our dream!

Notes from the Woodland's Heart

In the woods where squirrels dance,
Leaves play tricks in a leafy prance,
Whispers giggle, vines tease the breeze,
Mushrooms wearing tiny caps with ease.

Trees chuckle softly, a rustling sound,
Beneath their shade, funny creatures abound,
With acorns as hats and twigs as their canes,
Nature's jesters delight in their gains.

A rabbit hops wearing sneakers so bright,
While frogs in bow ties croak through the night,
The wind carries tales from root to high crown,
In this woodland circus, all turn upside down.

So grab a leaf, let the laughter unfold,
For in this green world, there's joy to be told,
With every rustle and playful retreat,
The heart of the woodland dances on feet.

Flora's Farewell

The petals waved goodbye with a grin,
As insects scampered, trying to win,
A dance-off with pollen, oh what a sight,
Nature's farewell, what a humorous plight!

The daisies wore shades, the tulips had flair,
They sang off-key, showing they care,
As wind blew their hairstyles, messy and wild,
Leaves giggled, calling each bloom a child.

Bumblebees buzzed, looking for tea,
While snails on a sidewalk danced slow with glee,
The sun grinned wide, spreading sunshine's glow,
A comedic farewell, with nature's best show.

In the fading light, laughter did swell,
As Flora's fans bid her fond farewell,
With a twirl and a giggle, the blossoms let go,
Creating a memory that still steals the show.

Pages from Nature's Book

In a book made of bark, tales swirl and spin,
Where rabbits tell stories of kitschy chagrin,
The chapters of leaves rustle with glee,
Each turn of the page is a new bit of spree.

A tale of a flower who fancied a bee,
Who wore polka dots and drank herbal tea,
They giggled and played through sunbeams of gold,
Leaving behind all their worries untold.

The mushrooms debated what color to wear,
While a wise old oak gave them quite the scare,
"Don't sweat the small stuff!" it bellowed with pride,
"Find joy in the rain and the moss by your side!"

With laughter and love, the pages unfold,
Nature's own stories, amusing and bold,
Each tale intertwined in the green world's nook,
With every slight breeze, more pages get shook.

Transformed by Time

Once a sprout, now a tree so wise,
From acorn to oak, what a surprise!
With branches outstretched, it cracks a loud joke,
"You won't believe how I avoided that choke!"

The daisies once laughed at the dandelions,
Now they're best friends, plotting alliances,
Together they giggle as children run by,
With crowns on their heads, oh my, oh my!

Leaves quip and chatter in colors so bright,
Trade wisdom for snacks in the soft moonlight,
"Let's make a salad!" one leaf did declare,
But no one had dressing—oh, what a despair!

As seasons change and the breezes sway,
The funniest stories are there to convey,
A romp through the forest, a whimsical climb,
A journey of laughter, all transformed by time.

Ashes of Green

Once a breeze made the trees laugh,
It tickled a twig, what a silly gaffe!
Leaves danced like fools in backyard delight,
Whispering secrets beneath moonlight.

One plopped in my soup, I took a big sip,
Tasted like dirt, what a fateful trip!
In the bowl of absurdity, they fit just fine,
A salad of giggles, quite a weird dine.

The branches conspired, set free their glee,
Chatting about acorns as if sipping tea.
All while I pondered, can leaves be friends?
Or are they just jokers from nature's blends?

So here's the tale of the leaves and their pranks,
Turning dull moments into wild flanks.
Mother Nature chuckles; oh, what a scene!
In the realm of the foliage, nothing's routine!

Celestial Shift in the Forest

When the sun does a twirl among branches so wide,
The shadows conspire, they dance side by side.
Mushrooms giggle as they sprout in surprise,
They're wearing hats made of autumn skies!

A squirrel with sass scales a trunk like an ace,
Flaunting his fluff in a leafy embrace.
He slips and he slides, what a sight I behold,
He yelps, 'I'm just testing my gold-plated bold!'

The owls take a selfie, they're posing just right,
Candid moments under starlit twilight.
They wink and they nod, such a wise little crew,
Saying, 'What a show—who knew they could stew?'

As the moon wobbles, the night takes its quest,
And leaves sing their ballads, the trees in their fest.
A chuckle in the woods, a giggle up high,
If you listen real close, they're all asking 'Why?'

Blades of Bronze and Gold

In a patch of sunlight, leaves play hopscotch,
Twirling and spinning, what a lively botch!
A blade of grass can be quite a delight,
Waving its arms like a dancer in flight.

"Who's got the moves?" shouts a leaf from the tree,
"Join me for spins, let's be wild and free!"
Choreographed chaos in a summer's green,
With roots that will giggle as the leaves preen.

The wind joins the party, a wacky old friend,
Making their frolic a whimsical blend.
"Watch out for the snail!' cries a twig with a grin,
"He dances like mad, let the fun times begin!"

Together they whirl, a wild leafy mess,
In the tapestry of nature, pure happiness.
So if you feel stuck in some mundane scroll,
Just glimpse at the leaves—they'll tickle your soul!

The Timeless Treetops

Up high in the canopy, the branches just sway,
Chatting with clouds in a whimsical way.
A curtain of laughter, they tumble and tease,
A ruckus of rustling, carried by breeze.

How many squirrels can fit in a tree?
They giggle and tumble, it's a sight to see!
They build their own kingdom, the cheekiest show,
With acorns for crowns, ruling high and low.

A woodpecker knocks on the trunk like a drum,
"Let's start a band!" he proclaims in the sun.
With leaves as the audience, they rock and they roll,
Nature's own rhapsody, funky and whole!

So let's tip our hats to the treetops so grand,
Where silliness blooms like a magical band.
For laughter's the language that they all recite,
In the forest of fun, everything feels right!

Adrift in a Sea of Leaves

In a swirling dance, they twirl around,
Making a mess on the picnic ground.
Squirrels laugh as they dive and leap,
While we all trip and land in a heap.

A leaf decides it's king for a day,
Leading us all in a leafy ballet.
With every gust, they tumble and shout,
Bidding farewell as they twist about.

Grabbing one for a quirky crown,
A gusty wind turns me upside down.
But in this chaos, I start to see,
The fun in leaves just wants to be free.

So here's to the rustle, the poke, and the shove,
Nature's confetti, a fit and a shove.
Adrift in this sea, I can't help but see,
Life's full of laughter, wild and carefree.

Ephemeral Echoes

Whispers of color, a giggle or two,
Leaves sharing secrets, just passing through.
One leaf tells jokes, another sings along,
The symphony of nature, a funny little song.

In the swaying branches, a comedy show,
The sunbeams laugh and the breezes blow.
When autumn's crisp hand gives one final shove,
They fall with a flair, like a clumsy dove.

Jumping on piles, I'm taken aback,
Each crackle and crunch fuels joyful crack.
As memories flutter with fabric so thin,
I giggle at leaves, where the laughter begins.

So here's to the moments that flutter and fly,
In the canopy's shade, we all reach for the sky.
A comical romp, with nature's sweet echoes,
Sailing on breezes, in living overflows.

Pages of the Wind

Fluttering pages, the wind writes a tale,
Of leaves on adventures, they never grow stale.
One leaf finds a hat, another a shoe,
In this wild park, where mischief brews.

The pages all flutter, each story unique,
A game of peek-a-boo, here they squeak.
From pine to oak, they leap and dive,
In the book of the breezes, they come alive.

Plot twists abound, on each branch they cling,
Falling in fits, like a clown with a spring.
With every gust, a laugh escapes,
As silly leaves take on silly shapes.

So here's to leaf volumes that twirl and sway,
In every rustle, there's humor at play.
We'll read every moment, a chuckle or two,
In the vibrant library of nature that grew.

The Whispering Canopy

Beneath the green roof, stories unwind,
Leaves share their secrets, oh aren't they kind?
One leaf is telling a joke to a pine,
While birches giggle in perfect time.

A chatter of rustles, a whispering spree,
Where branches gossip as wild as can be.
The canopy's laughter, so light and so free,
Paints a funny picture for you and for me.

When the wind starts to play, it's a rave in the sky,
Leaves wear their best, as they flirtily fly.
In this leafy salon, there's fashion galore,
With twirls and swirls, always wanting more.

So let's join the laughter, with roots in the ground,
In this cozy theater, our joy knows no bound.
With each gentle whisper, a chuckle will bloom,
Under the canopy's lighthearted room.

The Sound of Leaves Whispering

In the trees, a secret chat,
Leaves gossip, nature's spat.
Rustling tones of snickers fly,
As squirrels roll their eyes nearby.

A leaf fell down, with quite a thud,
Landing squarely in the mud.
The trees all chuckled, oh what fun,
They are the jokers, the chosen ones!

Underneath the boughs they tease,
Tickling twigs in playful breeze.
They share tall tales of sunny days,
While rustling softly in silly ways.

In a world of green and gold,
Whispers of wisdom, humor bold.
Nature's wit in every crack,
Leaves in laughter, never lack.

Kaleidoscope in the Breeze

Colors swirl like a wild dance,
A twist and turn, a playful prance.
Leaves in reds and yellows shout,
"Catch us if you can!" they pout.

The wind spins them with a grin,
A swirling show, let the fun begin!
They flip and flop, oh what a show,
Nature's circus, all aglow.

The oak tree says, "Don't be shy!"
As leaves do flips into the sky.
With every rustle, a joke unfolds,
Laughter's worth more than their golds.

A pirouette, a grand leap,
The leaves are secrets they must keep.
In the breeze, they twirl and tease,
Nature's jesters, all at ease.

Shimmering Gold beneath the Boughs

Golden leaves in the afternoon,
Giggle and shimmer, a sunny tune.
Rustling softly, they spin around,
Like little dancers on the ground.

Under the branches, a forest play,
Leaves turn bright at the end of the day.
"Look at us!" they proudly shout,
As squirrels nod, without a doubt.

With every gust, a new refrain,
Whispers of joy in the gentle rain.
The sunbeams offer a cheeky wink,
As leaves conspire, in friendship linked.

A chorus of colors, what a sight,
In their twirly whirl, they feel so bright.
A shimmer of gold in every glance,
Leaves lead the world in a merry dance.

Choreographed by the Wind

Beneath the breeze, the leaves unite,
A flick and flurry, oh what a sight!
Dancing lightly, a green ballet,
They put on shows in their leafy way.

Twisting and turning with every gust,
Trusting the wind, in fun they thrust.
An acorn laughs, saying, "Look at me!"
As leaves play pranks so mischievously.

The wind has taught them all its tricks,
A jolly routine of zig and zigs.
With every flap, a giggle's sparked,
Their joyful movements, brightly marked.

Under the sun's warm, teasing glow,
Leaves still giggle, row by row.
In each rustle, a joke will find,
Every leap is choreographed by the wind.

Leaf Songs

A leaf once sang a silly tune,
Dancing round beneath the moon.
It flipped and flopped through autumn's cheer,
Wiggling its stem, it had no fear.

With gusts of wind that made it glide,
It laughed and joked with branches wide.
"I'm not a salad!" it blared with glee,
"I'm a star on stage, come watch me!"

Each rustle spoke of leafy fun,
Sharing secrets like a pun.
A chorus formed; leaves joined in,
A concert sparked, let the fun begin!

They pranced and jived, a leafy show,
Each one boasting of where they'd go.
With every twist, they danced their laugh,
Accidentally crafting a leaf-path graph.

The Rhapsody of Rust

The rusty whispers of a leaf,
Told tales of joy beyond belief.
"Faded but bold, we dance around,
With colors bright, we touch the ground!"

In sepia tones, they twirled with flair,
A party happening without a care.
"I'm aging like fine wine, don't flee!"
"But don't forget, I'm still wily!"

They chuckled softly as they swayed,
In a vibrant dome of colors displayed.
Rustier jokes made their laughter bloom,
While swirling gold dust filled the room.

So sway along, embrace the fall,
It's not a funeral, it's a ball!
With every crinkle and crackled tune,
Leaves will conquer autumn's afternoon!

The Gentle Art of Fall

With a whoosh and a flap, the leaves descend,
They're tired of sticking, time to blend.
They swirl and twirl, a playful crew,
"Catch us if you can!" squealed each hue.

They play hopscotch on the breezy path,
With giggles that provoke Mother Nature's wrath.
"I'm not ready!" one leaf declared,
As its friends slipped, released, and fared.

Marvelous artistry in every spin,
Decomposing jokes beneath their skin.
"I'm no carpet, just give me a toss!"
Leaves leap with laughter, no time for loss.

So when you stroll and hear their cheer,
Join in the laughter, don't just steer.
With every fit of wind they call,
It's the gentle art of having a ball!

An Ode to the Fading Light

The sun bows low, a leaf's delight,
"Let's party hard, it's almost night!"
Its shadows stretch, a playful prank,
Leaves giggle softly, or so you'd think!

"We're not just shades of green, you know,
We're budding out in all this glow!"
Each golden beam a step to take,
As sunset brings a leafy bake.

The sky erupts in hues so grand,
Fabric of twilight, a magic band.
With winks and nods, they spark and play,
An ode to dusk, come seize the day!

As dusk descends with a playful crown,
Leaves laugh aloud amongst the brown.
"Endings are funny, light dims but brightens,
In our spirals, more mischief enlightens!"

Shadows of Autumn's Embrace

Leaves dance like clowns on the ground,
Chasing their shadows, round and round.
Squirrels dressed in coats so bright,
Plotting acorns in the fading light.

The pumpkins grin with goofy glee,
Whispering secrets of a leafy spree.
Rakes complain of the massive load,
While children laugh in a crispy road.

In the wind's song, there's a quirky jest,
As nature plays its comical quest.
A leaf slips and flies with flair,
Tickling the noses of those who dare.

When autumn hangs out and starts to tease,
Even the fog wears a funny sneeze.
So grab a latte, raise your mug,
For the wacky charms of the autumn hug.

The Grammar of Green

In the sentence of trees, punctuation leaves,
Commas of clovers, and photosynthetic thieves.
Adjectives swirl like breeze in a summer file,
While nouns giggle softly, it's all in style.

The periods are raindrops, plunking with cheer,
Conjunctions are worms that squirm far and near.
In the garden of syntax, a wild plot unfolds,
As green grammar grows with each story told.

"Hey there, leaf!" the ferns shout with pride,
"Don't be a leaf, just let loose and glide!"
With each eco-sentence, the world takes a pen,
Writing its saga again and again.

So plant your own phrases, let your colors pop,
With verbs of the winds, let your laughter drop.
For every green word is a giggle in bloom,
In this field of fun where silliness looms.

Secrets Stirred by the Breeze

Whispers revealed in a chirpy breeze,
About that time the branches tease.
A secret dance in the rickety trees,
While acorns gossip in playful freeze.

The grass tickles toes in a mischievous way,
Odd socks may wander where leafy kids play.
In a rustle of shrubs, there's laughter upheld,
Each leaf a pose in the stories they held.

The sun takes a bow while clouds play charades,
As shadows peek out from their leafy parades.
Breezes giggle, unraveling tales,
Of sneaky squirrels and their nutty travails.

So listen closely to the fluttering sound,
For laughter and secrets bloom all around.
Witty the world when leaves share their jest,
By the stirring of air, we are all truly blessed.

Ethereal Crumbles

A leaf's crisp crackle echoes delight,
As it plummets down in a wobbly flight.
With each little tumble, nature mimes,
In the dance of decay, with comical rhymes.

Mushrooms sprout like hats on the ground,
Winking at those who leap all around.
Fungi holding a laugh-a-thon bash,
With roots spinning tales in a leafy flash.

The wind playfully pokes at each bark,
Turning each tree into a quirky park.
With every crinkle, there's laughter to grasp,
In the crisp serenade of seasonal gasp.

So join in the fun of this earthy parade,
Where laughter and leaves never seem to fade.
With a sprinkle of whimsy in the air's gentle nudge,
The crumbles of nature whisper and trudge.

Revelations of Rustling Leaves

When leaves start to chatter, oh what a fuss,
They're gossiping trees, 'bout squirrels and thus.
"Did you see Fred's acorn?" one leaf does exclaim,
"He thought it was gold, but it's really just lame!"

In the breeze they giggle, a comedy show,
Whispers of secrets that only they know.
One leaf takes a tumble, falls right on a snail,
"Oops, sorry! Feeling hefty, like a leaf with a sale!"

Veins of the Earth

Roots wiggle and writhe in the cool, dark abyss,
Saying, "We're the veins, now who's getting the kiss?"
The worms roll their eyes like they're judging a scene,
"You think you're all cool? You're just all earthy green!"

The soil whispers back with a chuckle and grin,
"At least we have purpose, but you squirm and spin!"
Laughing together, the party goes on,
While shovels and rakes ponder seeds of a con."

Gold and Rust

In the fall, leaves flash colors that tease,
"Look, I'm like gold!" Then they rust in the breeze.
A twig shrugs, remarking, "You think that's a score?"
But wait for the winter, you'll be black and a bore!"

Golden hues twirl in a humorous race,
As they dance on the ground, and trip over space.
"Hey! Watch where you drop, you flashy old thing!"
Rust giggles back, "Just wait till spring!"

The Romance of Falling Petals

Petals float gently, like whispers of love,
"Catch me, oh breeze, I'm too pretty, my dove!"
But the wind just laughs, swirling them round,
"Hey, you're like confetti! Just look at you found!"

A flower blushes, and sighs with delight,
"I'm not just for parties, I'm sweet and polite!"
Then a bee buzzes close, with a wink and a grin,
"You're the belle of the ball; let the dance begin!"

Nature's Dance in the Twilight

At dusk, everything sparkles, a twinkling spree,
Leaves rustle and tumble, as merry as can be.
"Is that a cha-cha?" a branch starts to sway,
"Watch me do the tango!" a frond shouts in play.

The critters all gather, with paths now entwined,
"Let's boogie till sunrise! Nature's dance, combined!"
A raccoon tips his hat, with a wink and a spin,
"Who knew being leaf-y could lead to such win!"

Whispered Sonnets of the Evergreen

In forests green where squirrels dance,
The trees hold secrets, given a chance.
They giggle softly in the breeze,
While teasing branches bring you to your knees.

A leaf fell down, a tragic fate,
It pondered, 'Was I just too late?'
The acorns laughed, oh what a scene,
'You look like green confetti, so obscene!'

The pines are tall; they are quite grand,
But pinecone jokes? Not what we planned.
They roll their eyes at old oak's quips,
Trading barbs till the last leaf slips.

Beneath the boughs, woodland critters grin,
Knowing that laughter's where fun begins.
In this green realm, whimsy's the key,
So hear those whispers, come dance with me.

Harvest Moon and Treetops

Beneath the moon, the branches swayed,
In shadows deep, some mischief played.
The raccoons dressed in pumpkin hats,
   Judging the owls for their silly spats.

The apples blushed at the fox's praise,
   'We wear our skin like sassy spray!'
While leaves burst forth in vibrant tones,
   Singing of nights that chill our bones.

Squirrels trade nuts for the best of curry,
While mushrooms giggle in muddled hurry.
Grumpy old trees shake their twisted limbs,
'We're still the kings with our leafy whims!'

As friends unite for the harvest feast,
Even the crickets hum in the least.
Under the stars, with laughter so clear,
We toast to the sun, in their sizzling cheer.

Breaths of the Timbered Realm

In timbered halls, where whispers roam,
The barky statues call this home.
With chuckles echoed through the pine,
Even the moss shakes off the grime.

The rabbits rabbit on 'bout the best patch,
While owls debate who's the fiercest batch.
Meanwhile, the ferns give a shimmy and shake,
Knowing full well they can't make a mistake.

Beneath the oaks, a nutty debate,
'Who's there to cheer for the lilac crate?'
But laughter rises, as chatter collides,
In this hodgepodge of creatures and tides.

Naturally, trees just stand and stare,
As playful winds ruffle through their hair.
In the timbered realm, fun is a must,
So come crack a smile, in joy we trust.

Celestial Decay

Stars twinkled down on the leaves so bright,
While the woodpeckers drummed deep into the night.
'Pineapple' chirped in a hoot with flair,
As the moon rolled its eyes in ethereal care.

The cosmos yawned with leafy grins,
With twinkling dust as the party begins.
Jupiter's band took a cosmic turn,
While Saturn giggled at the moon's soft burn.

A comet whooshed with style so keen,
'Take that, earthlings, fresh in green!'
But oaks just laughed with a hearty cheer,
'Who needs space when we've got this sphere?'

With laughter echoing through voids so grand,
We celebrate time, both gentle and planned.
In the realm of decay, humor will stay,
As we dance, a cosmic ballet.

Fragments of the Fallen

A leaf in green tries to fit,
Screaming, "I'm fabulous, isn't it?"
Then a gust yanks it from its branch,
Doing a dance—oh, what a chance!

Once it twirled with style and grace,
Now it puddles in a muddy place.
It laments, "I'm not meant for this!"
"Could a squirrel just bring me bliss?"

In spring it dreamed of being whole,
Now it's a disc with a heart and soul.
It giggles, "What a twist of fate!"
„Could I still be a dinner plate?"

So if you see a leaf drop down,
Wipe the laughter from its frown.
It's a comedy of nature's jest,
Falling leaves are the very best!

Elemental Transformations

Once a bud, now a leaf with zest,
It gabs with worms and claims it's blessed.
"I'm a salad's crown, or maybe a wrap!"
But it flutters off—a weird mishap!

Late summer sun makes it turn bright,
"I'm a taco shell, what a delight!"
Then winter breath makes it brown and sad,
"I'm a potato chip, oh isn't that rad?"

Changing colors like a chameleon,
"I'm the rainbow's cousin, yes, a champion!"
But as the wind starts to blow,
"Oh no, not another show!"

It spirals down to join the team,
With acorns and dirt it starts to dream.
A leaf's life is a crazy ride,
Dressing up in seasons, full of pride!

The Canvas of Change

On nature's canvas, strokes collide,
Waves of greens that slip and slide.
"I'm a Picasso!" boasts the lime,
"Watch me paint in my prime!"

A red leaf giggles, "I'll add a flair!"
"Swirling oranges without a care!"
But as they tumble, they lose their stuff,
"Maybe colors are just too tough?"

A golden brown says, "I'm the fall's hero!"
While the wind replies, "You're just a zero!"
Yet they splatter all over the ground,
Creating laughter, all around!

When seasons change, the giggles spread,
Leaves fall and dance, no sense of dread.
In chaos, they find a happy tune,
A masterpiece that ends too soon!

Chasing Hues

A leaf once green played hide and seek,
"I'm going gold!" it started to speak.
It darted left and then to right,
"Catch me, squirrels, I'm taking flight!"

Then came a gust, a wild flurry,
Spinning fast, oh what a worry!
"Do I land with flair or above the muck?"
"I'd prefer a warm soup, oh what luck!"

As hues collide in crisp, cool air,
Each color shouts, with flair, with flair!
"I'm on a quest for my bright parade!"
But down they fell—an earthbound charade!

So when you chase the great outdoors,
Remember leaves will open doors.
They giggle, spin, in every hue,
Transforming dreams—just like you!

Chronicles of Change in the Canopy

Once a leaf had a dream,
To dance like a wiggly worm,
It twisted and spun on a beam,
And gave the squirrels a turn.

The oak laughed and shook its arms,
Said, "Join the breeze for some fun!"
The birch with its silvery charms,
Joined in till the day was done.

Maple jumped in with a splash,
Yelled, "Look at me, I'm on fire!"
But no one saw the mad dash,
As they tumbled like a choir.

Then came the wind, all a-woosh,
Sent them twirling around like a naughty twirl,
They wiggled and giggled in a gush,
Transforming the trees into a whirl.

The Symphony of Softly Falling Forms

In the forest, leaves hold a feast,
With the sun as their quirky host,
Each one was a shimmering beast,
Turned in air like a lively ghost.

The maples were playing the flute,
While oaks kept the tempo with clap,
Willows brought rhythm, oh what a hoot,
As they danced in their leafy cap.

Pinecones rolled in with a joke,
"Hey, don't forget us, we're a class!"
But no one could hear through the smoke,
Of laughter that whistled like grass.

As the leaves fell, they cheered and spun,
Creating a concert under blue skies,
In this goofy, leafy run,
Nature's jesters made joyful sighs.

Whispers in the Canopy

High up in the leafy heights,
The branches were gossiping fast,
"Did you hear about Nate and his flights?"
"Oh yes, but his landings never last!"

The maple piped in with a word,
"Said his buddy the tree stump fell twice!"
Their chuckles rang like a songbird,
As the wind caused mischief, so nice.

The birch whispered secrets so sweet,
"Who knew fern could wear a crown?"
Laughter echoed where branches meet,
As they dressed up the acorns in brown.

So if you listen close at dusk,
You might hear the leaves in a fit,
With tales of squirrels and a little husk,
Creating a forest-wide skit.

Transmuted Colors

Once there was a leaf so green,
Dreamed of becoming something grand,
It sought the magic of the scene,
To wear colors across the land.

"I'll try orange, red, and some gold!"
It yelled as it flipped in a spin,
"What fun to be bold, not just old!"
Making the other leaves grin.

The purple leaf tried to compete,
"I want sparkles, please turn me blue!"
And so they danced on nature's beat,
In hues that would make rainbows rue.

At last, every leaf turned a shade,
With laughter painting the trees,
Each color a joyous parade,
In a world that swayed with the breeze.

The Poetry of Dying Light

As sunlight fades, the shadows creep,
The leaves turn whispers, secrets to keep.
A squirrel in shades, with acorn bling,
Dances unaware of the winter's sting.

With giggles and chuckles from branches above,
The trees conspire, oh how they love!
To trick the winds, with a rustle and cheer,
A jest of the forest, let laughter draw near.

As twilight paints rays of golden delight,
The bugs take the stage in a comical plight.
Each flickering light feels like a tale,
Of fluttering mischief on a leaf-laden trail.

So here's to the dusk, with its funny charades,
Nature's wide grin as the daylight evades.
In every soft shadow, there's silliness too,
In the poetry of light that's fading from view.

Fluttering Secrets Beneath the Sky

Leaves are the gigglers, swaying in line,
They tickle the breeze, they sip on sunshine.
A rabbit's in costume, wearing a cloak,
Telling sweet stories that make the trees joke.

The sun winks low, with a mischievous gleam,
As clouds play tag, in a fluffy cream dream.
A ladybug lounges, on a bold, red seat,
Sipping on dew, a tiny, chit-chat treat.

Beneath the vast sky, fluttering sins,
Are whispers of creatures trying on fins.
The dragonflies giggle, spinning in flight,
A dance of pure chaos, a funny delight!

So, cheers to the laughter found in the trees,
Where secrets are shared by the buzzing of bees.
As time squirrels away, let's all have a laugh,
In fluttering whispers, where jokes will craft!

Nature's Whisper in Decay

When autumn arrives, there's a rustle and sigh,
As leaves offer secrets, and crickets comply.
The mushrooms pop in a polka-dot dress,
Inviting the spiders to dance and impress.

Each branch has a tale, with twists and with bends,
Of mischief and giggles, of trees being friends.
The acorns roll wild, in a comedic race,
Chasing the sun, oh, what a funny place!

As browning leaves flutter, in a flimsy ballet,
They twirl and they slip, come out to play.
With laughter that echoes in the crisp autumn air,
Nature's own secret, she dances with flair!

So let's raise a toast to this wacky display,
Where decay tells a story in a quirky way.
With every leaf falling, a joke in disguise,
Nature's great humor reflects in our eyes.

The Medley of Hues and Hush

A tapestry woven in reds and in golds,
Each leaf is a joker, with secrets retold.
The trees strip to laughter, in whimsical guise,
As colors collide in a colorful rise.

Hues play a game, and the wind joins the fun,
While twigs have a hoedown beneath the bright sun.
A chipmunk in shades, with a beret so fine,
Sips on a smoothie, with berries divine.

In the quiet of evenings, the colors all sway,
As whispers of red, slowly dance out of play.
The sunset chuckles, painting the skies,
With hues so vibrant, it brings joyful sighs.

So here's to the medley of colors that cheer,
A hush that holds giggles, a whimsical sphere.
Each leaf's little wink, as it flutters with grace,
Nature holds court, in this funny embrace.

www.ingramcontent.com/pod-product-compliance
Lightning Source LLC
Chambersburg PA
CBHW071814160426
43209CB00003B/82